Birds
Coloring Book for Adults
Doodle and Relaxing Patterns

Sophia Payne

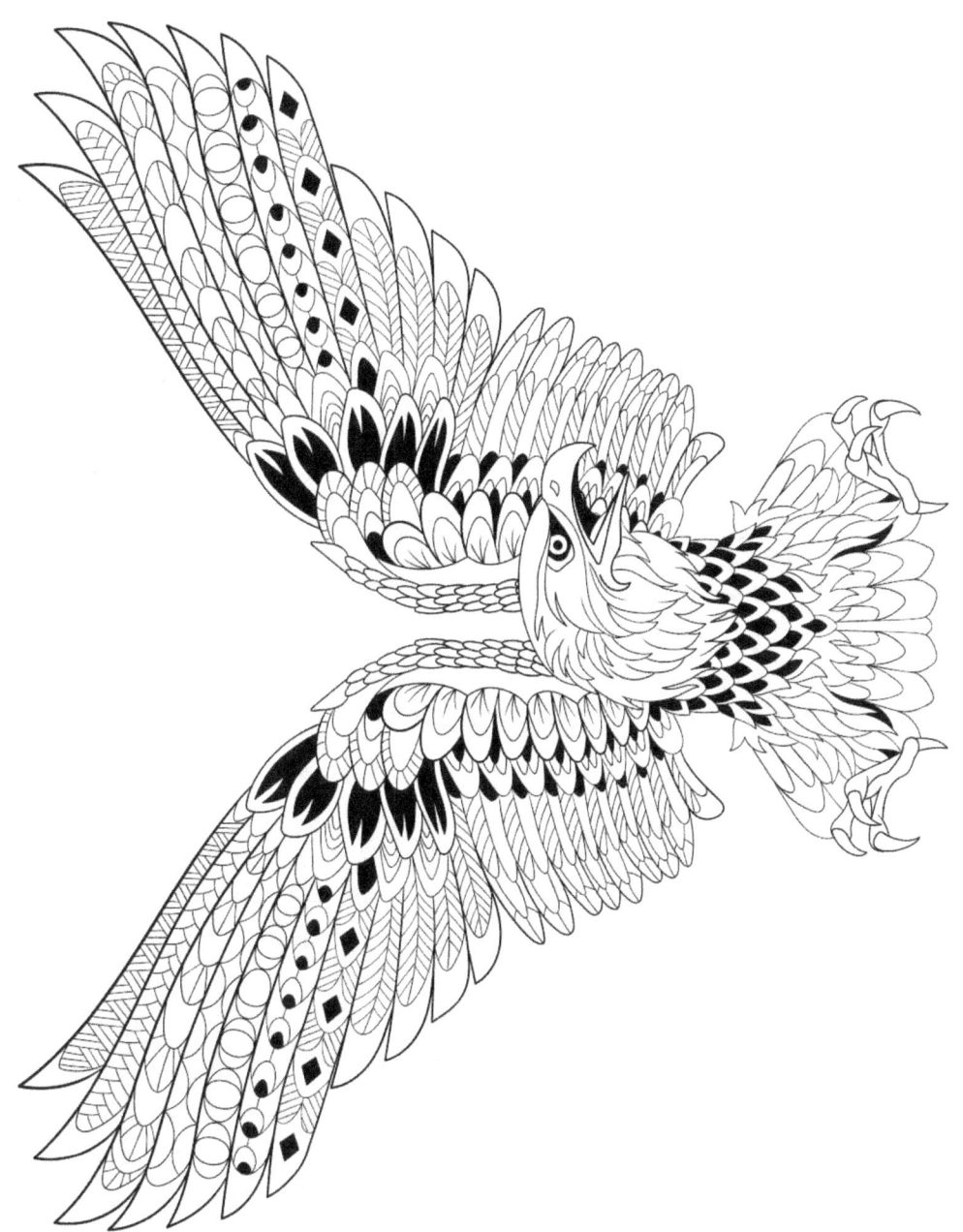

PDF Version this book : http://bit.ly/birds_c_1

Don't Miss Another our Books.

http://bit.ly/safari_coloring_b

ISBN : 9781523987931
(Use this ISBN for searching on amazon.com)

Join Us >> http://bit.ly/get_sample_free

- Get Free "Reviw Copies" of our New releases
- Exclusive offers and book giveaways
- More events from our community

Thank you